French Chic Living: The Ultimate Guide to a Life of Elegance, Beauty and Style

© **Copyright 2016 by Veronique Antoinette Blanchard - All Rights Reserved.**

This document is geared towards providing exact and reliable information with regards to the topic and issue covered. The publication is sold with the idea that the publisher is not required to render accounting, officially permitted, or otherwise, qualified services. If advice is necessary, legal or professional, a practiced individual in the profession should be ordered.

- From a Declaration of Principles which was accepted and approved equally by a Committee of the American Bar Association and a Committee of Publishers and Associations.

In no way is it legal to reproduce, duplicate, or transmit any part of this document in either electronic means or in printed format. Recording of this publication is strictly prohibited and any storage of this document is not allowed unless with written permission from the publisher. All rights reserved.

The information provided herein is stated to be truthful and consistent, in that any liability, in terms of inattention or otherwise, by any usage or abuse of any policies, processes, or directions contained within is the solitary and utter responsibility of the recipient reader. Under no circumstances will any legal responsibility or blame be held against the publisher for any reparation, damages, or monetary loss due to the information herein, either directly or indirectly.

Respective authors own all copyrights not held by the publisher.

The information herein is offered for informational purposes solely and is universal as so. The presentation of the information is without a contract or any type of guaranteed assurance.

The trademarks that are used are without any consent, and the publication of the trademark is without permission or backing by the trademark owner. All trademarks and brands within this book are for clarifying purposes only and are the owned by the owners themselves, not affiliated with this document.

Table of Contents

Introduction   4

Chapter 1 – Basics of Chic Living   6

Chapter 2 – Cultivate Pleasure and Beauty in Everyday Life   13

Chapter 3 – No Off Days for Beauty and Style   19

Chapter 4 – How to Take Care of Your Hair and Skin the French Way   23

Chapter 5 – Eat for Pleasure and Stay Slim for Life   26

Chapter 6 – Love Yourself   31

Conclusion   34

Introduction

In my first book, *French Chic: The Ultimate Guide to French Fashion, Beauty and Style*, I talked about how my mother's impeccable sense of style has had a definitive impact on my own personal sense of style. I also discussed how the years that I spent living in the US gave me a strong idea of the contrasts that exist between the two cultures while helping me understand why almost everyone seems to be fascinated by the French way of life.

Ultimately, this knowledge and understanding became my inspiration for creating the French Chic series. While my first book was primarily a guide to dressing like a French woman, this book is more about cultivating French Chic in all aspects of life.

As a native Parisian, I was fortunate enough to grow up witnessing how my mother or 'Maman' (as I called her) managed our household of four. There were so many things that I took for granted at that time. It was only when I had a family of my own that I realized how efficiently and seemingly effortlessly Maman had created a life of joy and beauty for us.

In this book, I have tried to include all the invaluable tips that you can incorporate into your own life to experience more pleasure and joy. Rest assured that all the information comes from my own experiences as a girl observing how her Maman did things and as a French woman living in Paris with a family of her own.

Needless to say, all the information that I have outlined in this book are things that I myself practice on a regular basis.

There are six chapters in this book, meant to be read over a period of six weeks. Each chapter ends with exercises for that week. Make sure that you do the exercises because that's what will really help you create the life you desire so much.

However, I understand that incorporating all the information you learn in each chapter might not be easy or even practical at first. I would suggest that you start out with at least one or two ideas from each chapter that truly inspire you and do those things for a week. Once they become a part of your life, pick out a few more ideas and incorporate those.

As French Chic Living is a way of life, you want to create lasting changes that truly transform you and your world. It's best to go slow but steady.

Therefore, it might be worthwhile to keep coming back to the book every now and then.

I would highly recommend that you read one chapter at a time. Incorporate the ideas of each chapter for one week before moving on to the next one. If you still want to read the entire book in a go, you are welcome to do so.

Nevertheless, I would still suggest that you do the exercises from each chapter over a period of six weeks so that you can get maximum value out of this book.

Now, without wasting any time, let's get started with the lessons in French Chic Living!

Chapter 1 – Basics of Chic Living

What does the word 'chic' really mean to you? To me, it means a kind of effortless beauty and mystery that some people or places seem to have. There is a sense of being perfect but seemingly effortlessly put together – a kind of aesthetical charm that enthralls and mystifies the observer even from a distance.

A vast majority of French women can be called chic. They have this aura of being beautifully put together without having made any effort. I have given a lot of thought and observation to this. In this chapter, I'll share with you what I have learned.

We will break down the basics of chic living to understand the fundamentals. Once you understand the fundamentals, it will be much easier to create a chicer life.

Mindfulness Equals Elegance

According to the Merriam-Webster dictionary, 'elegance' is a kind of 'refined grace.' Chic people and places are almost always elegant. But what exactly constitutes elegance? Let's explore together…

As you have probably seen and heard, we French take our food very seriously. It's quite unusual to find a French person running down the beautiful streets of Paris with a Starbucks in one hand while munching a croissant from the other. Instead, what you will find is people gathered at boisterous cafes with chairs facing the street.

This is probably one of the reasons why (might I dare say) Paris looks far more elegant than New York. There is a certain mindfulness that people infuse in their daily lives. What is the point of making all the money in the world if you can't even sit down to enjoy a cup of coffee while talking to the people who really matter most in your life?

From as far as I can recall, my family always had breakfast at the table. There would be conversation, laughter, discussions about social issues and about what each of us planned to do on that day. We'd always eat fresh food that Maman would lovingly prepare.

I really want you to understand the emphasis French people place on truly relishing every moment of life rather than just rushing through it. Trust me, when I am telling you that I never saw my parents hurry through life. They always woke up on time and gave themselves ample time to get ready. They always found time to talk to my sister and me at the breakfast table. Since we were brought up with these kinds of values, it naturally became an intrinsic part of my sister's and my personality.

Even though I have an extremely busy schedule with two kids, a husband, a part-time job, and a household to run, I make it a point to never rush. I wake up before my kids and husband do – it's the quiet time that I take out for myself every morning that keeps me grounded throughout the day.

I take my time to relish every moment of life even if I'm just vacuuming the living room. As mundane as it is, I view it as a sacred act of health-giving that keeps my family and me in good physical condition. When I'm making pastries for breakfast, I like to feel the texture of butter and flour as they mix together – the gooey deliciousness that results from the amalgamation of the two and the sheer sensual pleasure the very act of preparing the dough provides.

It's the everyday simple pleasures - the delicious aroma of coffee brewing, the buttery texture of a fresh croissant, the chirping of birds, the warmth of early morning sunshine, the laughter of children – that truly constitute joie de vivre. You don't need a big budget to live a French Chic life; what you really need is a taste for life. Even if you think you don't have it, you can surely train yourself to develop it.

It's very important to take your time to start the day on a positive and happy note. If it means, waking up earlier and going to bed earlier, then maybe that's what you must train your body to do.

When you wake up in the morning in a state of panic because you kept hitting the snooze button a tad too long, you are basically starting your day in a reactive mode. There is this sense of having everything spiraling out of your control.

Joie de vivre is the opposite of this – it's about graciously gliding through life as if you were making life happen to you instead of life happening to you.

Eliminate Clutter

Clutter is the enemy of chic. Having excessive possessions that are thrown around in a disorganized and disorderly fashion is truly the opposite of chic.

Growing up, our house wasn't particularly large but it was very well organized. We had fewer possessions than most American families do but each item was valued and loved. From how spick and span my parents kept our house, it was quite obvious how much pride they took in all their possessions and family heirlooms.

I think what really helped in keeping the house clutter-free was the fact that every item, whether it was big or small, had a designated spot. Each one of us was responsible for putting the items back in the exact spot. This simple technique made living clutter-free quite a breeze.

Another important factor at play was the fact that my parents didn't buy anything they didn't actually need. They saved for what they really wanted and once they acquired it, the item was valued forever. As a result of their own personal values, my parents trained us to use our money judiciously from quite a young age. If we wanted to buy something really bad, we had to save up for it.

They also taught us to always buy the best things we could afford even if it meant waiting quite a while before we could have it. As a result, I, like most French women prefer to buy the best that I can afford. In the grand scheme of things, this certainly translates to fewer possessions and a lot less clutter.

A lot of times, this means that I might have to delay the gratification of owning something I badly want as I have to first save up for it but this has been an excellent tool for keeping me away from impulse shopping.

In order to keep your wardrobe and house clutter-free, it's very important that you understand your own signature style. We discussed identifying your personal style in terms of your wardrobe choices in the first book. Here, I would urge you to identify, your personal style in terms of the kind of décor you like based on the same principles that you used for identifying your style of dressing.

I would suggest that you go through interior design magazines or Pinterest to find images that you absolutely love. What is the common theme in all of them? Are you attracted to modern designs with clean sharp angles or are you attracted to a more traditional décor with curve edges and sumptuous furnishings? Do you prefer the raw naturalness of French country style or the avant-garde rawness of industrial designs? We won't go that deep into identifying your personal style here but if you can create a vision board (whether on your wall or your computer), you can have a great guide for keeping your home and all your shopping in alignment with your personal sense of style.

Once, you have nailed down your style, you will be less likely to buy items you don't really need. For instance, if your personal décor style is traditional European, then, even if you come across the most magnificent flower vase that looks very modern, you'd know that it won't go with the rest of your house's décor and is, therefore, not a smart purchase. Before making any purchase, it's important to make sure that the item can fit in with the rest of your house or wardrobe.

One of the best books that I would suggest for mastering the art of de-cluttering is *'The Life-Changing Magic of Tidying Up.'* Japanese de-cluttering expert, Konmari, teaches the method that has helped thousands of people get rid of clutter from their homes and lives. I would suggest that you start by getting rid of everything that you don't really need and those things that don't make you happy. Also, if you haven't needed something in 2 years, then you will likely never need it again!

Manage Your Time and Organize Your Life

My mom was a natural when it came to time management. She never left dirty dishes in the sink or forgot to put on her lipstick for that matter. As a grown-up, when there are days I feel overwhelmed with my never-ending to-do lists, I often wonder how my mom managed to look so calm and composed while going through the most demanding of days.

I think it all boils down to the fact that she was an excellent time manager. She had a day and time for everything.

Another one of her secrets was that she added joy to every mundane activity by turning them into rituals. For instance, Saturdays were reserved for laundry. Each one of us sorted through our through our clothes and had to separate the whites from the colored clothes. My mother would then wash the clothes. Once the washing was done, my mother, sister and I will fold the clothes while happily chatting about life. This is how something mundane and what can be incredibly boring to a lot of people became an opportunity for us to socialize and share moments of togetherness.

If you have a family, then you can create rituals around mundane tasks. If you live alone, you can still build your own rituals. After all, a ritual is nothing but a series of activities performed in a prescribed order. Having daily, weekly, monthly and yearly rituals will help you feel more grounded in life. You'll know exactly when you need to do something instead of just reacting to the demands of life.

Moreover, the fact that my mother never left any task unfinished helped her retain the unfazed calmness she always had. When you finish the tasks you take up, you get a sense of accomplishment. This not only boosts your confidence and self-esteem but also empowers you with a strong sense of having things under your control.

Surely, you can't control everything in life but you can definitely control how you react to everything. If you are proactive with your planning and time management, then you won't encounter many situations that catch you off guard.

Exercises for Week 1:

Add a Little Elegance and Mindfulness

1. Go to bed and wake up on time every day so that you can enjoy a wholesome breakfast with your family or by yourself (if you live alone). If, for some unforeseen reason, you get delayed for bed, make it a point to still wake up on time the next day. Would you prefer being a little sleep-deprived or feeling like you have been hit by a tornado? It's much better to catch up a short nap in the afternoon and retire to bed much earlier than your designated bedtime on that day.

2. Make sure that you add some leisurely time in the morning for doing something you truly enjoy – it could be a long bath, a walk in the park, having coffee at your favorite café, making love to your spouse or just about anything that gives you joy. When you start the day on such a high note, you are almost guaranteed to have an amazing day. Therefore, give yourself time to warm up to the day by starting out with something you love doing.

3. Whether you are having lunch or walking down the street, do everything by being fully present in the moment. We all have endless to-do lists but there's only so much you can do at one time. Thinking about the scary meeting you are going to have with your boss while walking down the belle rues of Paris is anything but pointless. It can only make you feel negative, and, likely, attract negativity into your life. Instead, immerse yourself in the beauty that surrounds you – rejoice in the chirping of birds, the laughter of children, and everything beautiful. Focus on what's good and what you can be grateful for in every moment.

Attack Clutter

1. I'm not expecting that you'll get rid of all the clutter from your life within a week but, this week, at least make an attempt to start out somewhere. Maybe, it's your wardrobe you want to tackle first or your kitchen. It's up to you but de-clutter at least one area of your life or house.

2. From now on, always identify a place for things and make sure that you put everything back at the same spot every time. Train your family to do so as well (I understand that this is not going to be very easy but over time, they will start becoming receptive. Don't lose patience – it takes time for new habits to form.

3. Create a vision board to represent your ideal house. Make mental notes of the décor style you like and use the board as a reference manual every time you decide to buy anything for your house.

Manage Your Time and Organize Your Life

1. Start scheduling out your week and every day in advance.

2. Identify all the big things you need to get done and designate a day and time for each activity. Try to stick to the schedule as much as possible.

3. Anticipate any interruption you might have and make room in your schedule for those.

4. Don't forget that effective time management is all about being in control of your time. Don't allow yourself to become overwhelmed by the schedule you have set by panicking about every 5-minute delay. Do your best to stick to the schedule but be lenient with yourself if you aren't able to get each task done within the time frame you had set. The schedule is only there to help you get the most out of life. It's a blueprint for success and happiness which, if followed, will give you great results but it's not set in stone either.

Chapter 2 – Cultivate Pleasure and Beauty in Everyday Life

Life is a precious gift. However, sadly, most people never take the time to feel grateful for everything they have. They are constantly in a rut for more – never stopping to appreciate the beauty of everything they already have. Please don't forget that joy and pleasure do not come from having more, it comes from appreciating what you already have. You don't need to achieve big things in order to live a happy life. You simply need to become present in the here and now to fill your days with beauty.

Ralph Waldo Emerson famously said, "Love for beauty is taste, the creation of beauty is art." I urge you to turn your life and every day in it into a work of art. Yes, it's possible, and yes, you can do it. You are the director and the writer of your life's movie.

No matter where you are living at the moment or what your current life situations are, you have the power to add pleasure and beauty to your life right now. Remember, life is too short to spend doing anything other than enjoying it. Therefore, enjoy all the chores you have to do, enjoy the job that you have, enjoy the family life you have, enjoy taking care of yourself – of your house, of your kids, of your laundry, of your garage, of everything.

The Simple Pleasures of Life

My parents had a record player that they loved playing every morning while getting started for the day. I would witness Maman joyously prepare breakfast to the beautiful renderings of Bach and Chopin. This was a source of such immense joy to my family and me that to this day, I fondly remember those idyllic mornings.

I have always felt that classical music has a way of elevating the mundane to the exquisite. There's something magical and incredibly refined about it. I don't have a record player but to keep our family tradition alive, I do love to play classical music on my music player every morning.

Even if classical music just isn't your thing, you can add your favorite music to the background as you are getting ready for your day or finishing it. Music touches the soul – it has the ability to envelope the most mundane moments in a glittering wrapper of graceful beauty.

I think Maman genuinely understood the power of music. Therefore, she'll always have a beautiful composition playing in the background – it didn't matter whether she was cleaning the floor, polishing the numerous family heirlooms we owned or simply relaxing on her bed.

Here, I must also mention that Maman would take pride in everything she did. She never looked frustrated or flustered in the least. She would do everything as if it were the most glorious and dignified task on the planet while Tchaikovsky or Beethoven played there greatest compositions in the background. I often wondered if it was music helped her elevate the ordinary to the exquisite.

Talking more about everyday joys and simple pleasures – I took notice of the fact that my parents always kissed each other before they went anywhere without the other. It was their ritual – such a simple but glorious way of acknowledging their love and affection for each other!

Other simple pleasures in our life included always having our breakfast and dinner together at the table. My parents always made it a point to leave the stresses of their life behind while spending time with us. They would choose to forget the rest of the world, being fully present with us and the food on the table as we spent the mornings and evenings chatting about everything under the sun.

My parents always put the needs of the family first. For them, spending time with us and our extended family was the most important thing in the world. I fondly remember languorous picnics with my parents and sister when everything in the world seemed to just be perfect. Then, there were those boisterous family reunions when our entire extended family will come together to celebrate a special day or just life.

What I learned from my early years was that true pleasure lies in enjoying the company of those who love us and those whom we love. Everyday pleasure is all about making time for your loved ones – to sit with them, to spend time with them, to hear what they have to say, to show them what they mean to us.

Unfortunately, we have become so preoccupied with our fast-paced lives that we often lose sight of what's truly important. Think about it – in the end, it won't matter which car you drove or which handbag you owned. Instead, people will remember you for how you made them feel. Real happiness and true pleasure come with loving others with all our heart and rejoicing in the warmth of our shared affections.

Just like our morning rituals, our family had a nighttime ritual as well. Instead of the whole family sitting in front of the TV as most families do today, we'd do something that would strengthen our bond. Not that I understood things at such a deep level back then but looking back, I have a better understanding of the values my parents wanted to inculcate in us. I still fondly remember the ecstasy I felt every night that we spent playing Scrabble, Dominoes or Monopoly. There were several other games that we played together but these are the ones that stand out in my memory most as they were my favorites. On the other hand, when my sister and I had our examinations, my parents would sit with us, helping us prepare for the next day. The point was that it wasn't what we did that mattered most but the fact that every activity we did together brought us closer to one another.

Twice a year, we also had the tradition of going on a family holiday. We'd often just travel to another place in France or sometimes to Europe. Again, it wasn't what we did or where we went that mattered as much as the fact that we were spending time together.

With my family now, I try my best to follow in the footsteps of my parents – creating a positive and nurturing environment for everyone. In our home, we have serious restrictions on how much TV time is allowed for both adults and kids. I like to involve my kids and husband in many of the activities we do at home. Like, if I am baking pastries, I ask my kids to help with the dough or get them involved with setting the table at dinnertime.

Beauty in Everyday Life

You don't have to live in a grand chateau in order to surround yourself with soul-stirring aesthetical beauty. In fact, beauty is something that you can cultivate and create. The only thing that is needed is a desire to do so.

I remember very well the transformation that Maman created for one of our relatives. A distant relative of ours, who wasn't very well off financially, had moved in into a new house. She was living with her husband and a five-year-old son. The new house was quite old and nothing more than purely functional. One day when she came to visit Maman, she narrated how sad she was about the condition of her new house. She didn't feel like taking care of it as, according to her, it looked filthy and ugly. Maman was always someone who wouldn't miss an opportunity to help someone so she offered to help transform the house for our relative within a budget that was comfortable to her.

I was 12 years old at that time. I remember going to the relative's house and the sheer sense of shock I felt at the contrast between our orderly and beautiful house versus the relative's unkempt chaotic house. Within a week, Maman had waved her magic wand.

In the course of the week, she had taken the relative to discount stores, flea markets, and charity shops to buy home furnishings. The house was repainted by their family and ours. There was fresh wallpaper on the walls, beautiful rugs, and other delightful furnishings sourced at bargain prices. The transformation of the house was quite extraordinary – it had become a gentle and warm haven for the soul.

You see the point I am trying to make here? It's not about how much money you have but how well you use your taste to create beauty around you!

Another thing that I loved about my parents was that they always looked presentable. I think my mother would be horrified at the idea of wearing sweatshirts and sweatpants around the house or anywhere for that matter! I always saw her dressed in her best clothes every single day. The same was true for my father.

In general, my parents always used their best things for everyday life; whether it was their finest clothes or their precious China. This is what real luxury is all about. It's not about owning more nice things but about regularly using the best things you own.

Now, if you are like most people, you'd say what if I ruin them? My question is how many times in a week do you really ruin your clothes no matter what kind of tasks you are doing? Or how many times have you broken your crockery? If you are like most people, then these are things that rarely happen to you.

Who knows whether there will even be a tomorrow or not – why keep your best for the last when you don't even know how long your life is going to last! Live each day as a celebration. Look and feel your best – take pride in everything you have and own.

Don't forget that the most precious thing in life is life itself!

Exercises for Week 2

1. Always eat each meal at the table. If you live with your family, then try to get your family to sit together at every meal without any distractions (have strict rules for no TV, no laptops, and cellphones at the dining table).

2. Play some classical music (or whatever your favorite kind of music is) in the background while you are getting ready or doing daily chores. Imagine yourself as the lead actress in the movie of your life. Let every action you do come from a place of beauty and grace.

3. Take pride in everything that you are doing throughout the day. Treat each task as if it was the most glorious and dignified task on Earth.

4. Make time for doing something that bonds your family together. Develop some kind of morning and evening rituals that you all can do together.

5. Get your family involved in helping you out as you complete chores around the house.

6. Make time for yourself. Do your best to look presentable at all times.

7. Think about ideas to beautify your home and your environment. It doesn't have to involve spending a lot of money. Imagination is the key here.

8. Be sure to stick by the no clutter tolerance rule this week and in all the following weeks as well.

Chapter 3 – No Off Days for Beauty and Style

Maman looked presentable every single day. While growing up, I took this for granted. It was only after my time in the US that I began to truly appreciate the values that my mother represented and had inculcated in me.

Because of my upbringing, I had learned quite early in life that looking presentable at all times was important.

I think part of the reason why Maman always looked presentable was that she knew exactly what her style was. She never had to go through those days of "Oh, I have a closet full of clothes but nothing to wear." She was a smart shopper. Every time she went to the store, she knew exactly what she wanted. She hardly ever made impulse purchases. Her style was feminine and graceful. She usually wore a simple skirt that fell slightly below her knees and a soft delicate-looking blouse. She would put her hair up in a French knot and apply a swipe of red lipstick along with some smudged eyeliner. That was her signature look. For special occasions, she might make a few variations but she never deviated dramatically from her signature style.

Since she was so strongly in touch with who she was as a person and what her signature style was that getting dressed every morning remained a simple affair for her. At home, in the mornings and at night before retiring to bed, she would also wear beautiful robes. Those were times when she would leave her shoulder-length hair loose. However, she was a living embodiment of elegance and femininity at all times.

I make it a point to also look my presentable best. To me, it's not a chore but something I take a lot of pleasure and delight in doing. It's a habit that has become deeply ingrained in my psyche.

If you also want to look immaculate at all times, then it is very important that you understand who you are as a person. Without this knowledge, you cannot build a wardrobe that seamlessly matches your personality and lifestyle.

If you need help building a classic French wardrobe and haven't already read the first book, French Chic: The Ultimate Guide to French Fashion, Beauty and Style, then, I would suggest that you refer to it. Once you have built a timeless wardrobe that reflects your personal sense of style and is not dependent on style trends, you will find it much easier to get dressed every morning.

I would also suggest investing in a beautiful robe for those days when you want to laze around the house. Lazing around in a robe is far from elegant than doing so in a tattered t-shirt and sweatpants. It's also very elegant to wear a robe on top of your nightie as you walk around the house at night and in the early mornings.

Whenever you are feeling low or not too happy, let me ask you to do something: take out your favorite dress in which you look like a million bucks and wear it. Don't worry about ruining – just wear it.

Even if you are just sitting around the house, you will automatically start to feel better. The reason why this works is because how we feel about our life and how we treat our own self are two strongly correlated things. When you don't take care of yourself or care to look your best every day, you are sending out a subconscious message to your mind that you are not worthy of your own time. Therefore, take time to care for yourself and do your best to look your best every single day.

Most people make the mistake of thinking that they have to look presentable only when they are going out in public. What is it that really matters – how other people perceive you or how you feel about yourself? When you spend the majority of your life at home, then doesn't it make sense to look your best even at home? Aren't you important enough for yourself to look presentable even if the only pair of eyes that are going to see you are your own in the mirror?

I would say it is totally worth the effort. This is what true Chic living is all about – who you are in private is the same person as who you are in public. Think about it, would you wear old crumpled clothes going to a five-star restaurant? Likely, not. If you want to turn your home into a haven for your soul, then you must treat yourself as the goddess who inhabits that paradise.

Also, don't forget that it takes exactly the same amount of time to put on a beautiful silk blouse as it does to put on a tattered t-shirt. Another amazing thing you will notice is that it will become easier for you to sit straight when you are dressed your best. You will stand taller and walk with pride.

Chic living is not about looking good or having a beautiful home to impress other people. It's about looking your best and living in the most beautiful house you can create so that YOU can truly get the most joie de vivre.

Life is too short – make it beautiful and absorb all the beauty that surrounds you.

Exercises for Week 3

1. Make a pledge to look presentable every single day of this week without taking any time off. If you start to enjoy this, then make sure to continue with this forever! However, for now, and because our mind likes the idea of deadlines, aim for dressing your best this entire week.

2. Be sure to wear your best clothes. I'm not suggesting you take out your silk evening gown but the silk blouse you absolutely love and that makes you feel like a million bucks, totally yes.

3. Start making efforts to build a classic wardrobe that reflects your style and personality. Again, refer to French Chic: The Ultimate Guide to French Fashion, Beauty and Style, if needed.

4. Do something to celebrate each day. If that means, ending the day with a relaxing bubble bath, then go for it. Or, if like me, you would like to maintain a gratitude journal, then do that. The idea is to do something that exhibits the gratitude you feel for your life and everything in it. The more grateful you feel, the more blessings and good fortune you attract in your life.

5. Try to find a night robe that you can wear around the house when you aren't fully dressed. It's totally worth investing in a gorgeous robe – you will feel amazingly sexy and put together in it!

Chapter 4 – How to Take Care of Your Hair and Skin the French Way

Most French women prefer what is popularly known as 'lived in hair.' If you don't know what this term means, then let me define it for you. This is the effortless 'I don't care and I can't be bothered' hairstyle that most French women have. It isn't styled to perfection and is, in fact, quite the opposite. The iconic French style is all about looking effortlessly gorgeous – as if you woke up looking like a goddess.

French women don't normally use hairdryers and too many products or appliances. As far as Maman is concerned, I never saw her use a hairdryer. I don't think she even owned one! She had slightly wavy hair which she allowed to air-dry every time she washed it. She washed her hair once a week, usually on Friday nights. She would do it in the evening as going out with wet hair in public is a big no-no in France. Her routine was really quite no-fuss. She used a hydrating shampoo and conditioner that was suitable for her thick hair. Every fifteen days she would apply an egg white and honey mask to her hair and then wash off the mixture with shampoo and conditioner.

Maman had beautiful skin. Even in her sixties, she didn't have any wrinkles. Her beauty routine was also very simple. She followed the simple cleansing toning and moisturizing routine that most French women swear by.

Maman had a strong preference for natural chemical-free products. Her routine was simple and only 3 products were required for it. She would always buy the best products she could afford. Before buying, she always did her research and tried out samples. When she finally found something that worked for her, she remained loyal to it.

Once a week, she would also prepare a face mask made with mashed grapes, olive oil, and honey. She used to tell me that it was excellent for keeping skin nourished and hydrated. I can vouch for the fact that it worked because she always looked radiant with glowing luminous skin. I have since kept the tradition in my own beauty routine and I can vouch for the fact that it really works!

My mother also went for regular facials. She would usually go on a Saturday afternoon once a month. She had a trusted facialist on whom she relied for all her skincare needs. When I was older, I asked her to take me to the lady for a facial and sure enough that woman weaved some magic into my skin.

When it comes to makeup, Maman like most French women preferred a minimal makeup look. You'll hardly find any French woman wearing heavy foundation or excessive makeup in general. Instead, the emphasis is on maintaining healthy skin and hair.

One makeup item a lot of French including my mother and myself love is red lipstick. To me, it's the perfect accessory to go with any outfit. I instantly feel more put together the moment I swipe my favorite red lipstick.

In general, French women prefer a natural look. They would much rather invest in good health and overall wellness than in revolutionary cosmetic enhancements.

However, it's true that despite all the fresh food and healthy lifestyle, a lot of French people smoke. Due to this many French women might suffer from sallow lifeless skin. My parents, however, were very much into living a healthy lifestyle. They neither smoked nor did they drink much. They also went to bed on time and woke up early every day. I think it was their healthy lifestyle and staying true to their culture that kept them looking their best even well into their seventies.

Exercises for Week 4

1. Create a custom skincare routine that is suitable for your skin and follow it religiously.

2. Don't go to bed without removing your makeup completely. Make it a point to complete your skincare routine no matter how tired you are. Your skin will really thank you for this!

3. Try to wash your hair only once (or at the most, twice) a week. At first, your hair might feel excessively greasy but over time, it will become accustomed to producing less oil.

4. Get a facial. Find someone who uses natural products and knows about acupressure points. Give yourself this gift because you deserve it! If you enjoy it, then try to make it a part of your regular monthly routine.

5. Try out the grape and honey mask. Mash 7-8 grapes into a pulp and add $1/4^{th}$ teaspoon olive oil along with $1/4^{th}$ teaspoon honey. Cleanse your face and neck first, then, apply the mask. Leave the mixture on your face for 20-25 minutes and then wash off. Pat dry and voila! However, if you have oily skin, you might want to skip the oil. Instead, you can add a few drops of lemon juice. For acne prone skin, add a few drops of tea tree oil instead.

6. Try out the minimal makeup look and see how it works for you. You might not be comfortable ditching the foundation instantly but over time, as your skin becomes more radiant and luminous, you might want to do so.

7. Follow a regular sleep schedule and try to make healthy choices in your everyday life. For instance, take the stairs instead of the elevator. It's the small changes that create the greatest transformations.

8. Find your perfect shade of red lipstick and wear it for at least a day. (Optional. But if you really want to channel your inner French diva, then don't skip this one)

Chapter 5 – Eat for Pleasure and Stay Slim for Life

You have likely already heard that we French love our food with an ardent passion. In fact, a lot of social activities in France are always planned around good food and fine drinks. Most French people cannot even imagine a diet of broccoli and boiled meat. We love our cheese, butter, and cream. If you are like everyone else, then you have also wondered how the French manage to stay slim despite eating all the rich food.

The secret lies in portion control. Since we eat good food that satisfies our taste buds as much as it satiates our hunger, we don't feel the need to go overboard. A small piece of cheesecake laden with flavor and deliciousness is enough to satisfy a French person. Also, there is a strong emphasis on using the best and highest quality ingredients sourced from local markets.

When I first arrived in the US, I was absolutely shocked by the portion sizes. I didn't understand why restaurants always serve more food than what people can comfortably eat. Also, in American society food is seen as a necessity and very much a hassle instead of something that gives joy. Most Americans don't take the time to prepare their meals and even when they do so, they usually use canned ingredients to prepare the dish.

Like most French people, my parents loved shopping for their groceries and making their own meals. We would often have small gatherings at our house and I would watch my mother joyously prepare a selection of delicacies.

After all, love for good food is part of the French cultural heritage. For us, good food and cooking delicious meals is a celebration of life rather than a hassle.

How to Stay Slim and Enjoy All the Good Food

If you want to stay slim and enjoy all the French delicacies, then you must learn something which is hardly a secret: self-control combined with portion control. If portion control is too difficult for you, then, at least, try switching to smaller plates and bowls. This way you can visually trick your subconscious mind into believing that you have the same amount of food on your plate as earlier when it's actually just an illusion.

Also, you have to stay away from fad diets. French women don't live on a slice of grapefruit and coffee. They love life and they understand that good food is one of the most basic pleasures of living well.

However, they also don't eat past their hunger. Once you have finished the serving you have on your plate, take some time before you reach out for another helping. The reason is that it takes about 20 minutes for your brain to receive the signal that your stomach is full. You could very easily overeat if you don't estimate your body's needs correctly.

A thumb size rule I personally follow is to not eat more than a fistful at any meal. As delicious as something is, the real richness and deliciousness lie in the very first bites of that food. After a few minutes, your taste buds become saturated and you don't get the same kind of satisfaction eating it. I would, therefore, advice that you eat slowly and mindfully. Avoid reaching out for another helping. If you start feeling weak in the knees, then just ask yourself if a few bites of superficial pleasure are worth the guilt you are going to feel afterward. It will take some time for you to develop self-control but over time, and with practice, you will surely get there.

Also, please remember that we don't eat desserts at every meal. Usually, either there would be no dessert on a regular weekday lunch/dinner or you'll be served something healthy like fresh fruits and yogurt. It's also unusual for the French to snack in-between meals. Mealtimes are fixed and everyone waits for food to be properly served at the table.

So if you are trying to lose fat from the body, then cut down portion sizes. Don't eat more than a fistful at any meal. This might not be easy at first but over time, your body will get accustomed to the new habit because overeating is also a habit. Most people, especially in the US, tend to overeat without even realizing that they are doing it. If you continue to feel hungry, then wait for at least 20 minutes before serving yourself another portion. Even then, remain conservative with your portion sizes. After a while, you will realize that most of the time what you feel is mental hunger and not actual physical hunger.

I would urge you to also cut down on all processed and packaged food completely. No matter how busy you are, it is possible to prepare something healthy or buy something healthy that is freshly prepared. Fix your mealtimes and ALWAYS eat at a table. I can't emphasize this enough. If you are eating while running errands or by sitting in front of the TV, then it's very easy to become completely disconnected from your body's needs. You'll end up eating more than you actually need while also not being able to relish your food.

If you'll stick to eating three wholesome meals a day, then you won't really feel the need for snacking but if you do get really hungry in-between meals, then I would suggest having a fruit with some nuts or yogurt. Also, if dessert is your weakness and you just can't seem to give up on it, then try to replace it with healthier options that can satisfy your sweet tooth. For instance, you can bake an apple or pineapple and serve it with some honey. In short, try to make a dessert with fruits without adding any sugar, butter or cream to it.

Once you have attained your desired body shape, you can have your favorite desserts in reasonable portion sizes. Once you have established the habit of eating with restraint and pleasure, it will be easier to not over-indulge.

The Exercise Secret

You probably already know this and if you don't, then let me tell you the truth: French women don't go to gyms. They stay in shape by remaining physically active throughout the day. Most French people walk everywhere, whether it is to work or to shop for daily necessities. Also, since one has to go to different specialty stores to source the various items on one's grocery list, this ensures quite a lot of walking.

I would encourage you to take up a more active lifestyle instead of doing extremely intense that you can't actually stick with for the long-term. Walk as much as you can. In fact, find reasons to walk every day. If you live in a city where it's impossible to walk everywhere, try parking your car a block away from your destination or maybe you could build up a schedule to go walking at the nearby park every day. If you are among those people who find it difficult to take up any physical activity alone, then I would suggest trying an audiobook for company. Imagine how much good you could do to your body and mind by going for walks while listening to an audiobook from which you have valuable things to learn.

Walking is pretty much the only exercise French people do on a regular basis. On a typical day, I find myself walking for at least an hour. I don't go the gym or engage in other forms of exercise as I already have a very busy schedule. I can admit that I am in great shape overall.

I would suggest that you try out the principles highlighted in this chapter and see for yourself if they work for you.

Exercises for Week 5

1. Time you meals and stick to the timings as much as you can.

2. Eat your food at the table.

3. Eliminate snacking. Every time, you feel hungry, try drinking some water or herbal tea. After a while, your body will adapt to your new eating habits.

4. If you absolutely must eat something in-between meals, then eat a fruit and/or some nuts/ yogurt.

5. Control portion sizes. Avoid eating more than a fistful at any given meal.

6. Replace desserts with fruit. However, don't deprive yourself too much. Allow yourself to indulge once a week (but keep the portion sizes under control).

7. Walk everywhere as much as you can. If it's not possible, then, at least, park your car a block away from your destination.

8. Go for regular walks to your nearby park. To keep it fun and to also to get maximum value out of your time, try listening to an audiobook while walking.

Chapter 6 – Love Yourself

In France, there is a lot of emphasis on staying natural. You won't find too many women with botox, fillers, implants or other cosmetic enhancements. In fact, I never saw my mother get any of these or for that matter any of my other relatives. Everyone in France (at least, the vast majority) prefer to embrace their natural beauty while making the most of their God-given features.

My mother did not color her hair even after she started graying. Instead, she embraced the greys in a chic Parisian bob. Although it's not like French women would steer clear of just about any kind of artificial beautification, the norm is usually to embrace the body as it is. Even when women color their hair, it's very subtle close to their natural hair color.

However, I am not suggesting that you can't color your grey hair or turn your blond hair into a chestnut brown. The point that I am trying to make here is that you are perfect the way you are. If colored hair is your thing, then do it. If it's not, then don't let society dictate to you how you should wear your own hair.

The more fully you embrace yourself, the more other people will accept you for who you are.

Also, don't worry too much about being impossibly perfect all the time – it's okay to have slightly messy hair or a little sweat on your skin. French women don't (well, at least, they pretend to not fuss too much over these things.

Feel good inside and you will always look impeccable outside. How you feel about yourself is the most important ingredient for looking your best every day. After all, confidence is the best accessory.

If you'll visit any popular beach in France, you'll find plenty of women baring 'it all.' It's not as much for a tan as much as it is about being comfortable with the natural state of the body. Let me tell you that your body is beautiful and perfect the way it is. Look at it as a magnificent machine that allows you to have a rich and diverse experience of life. Love it for what it does for you 24x7 without expecting anything in return.

Therefore, embrace yourself for who you are and don't be afraid to show your truth to the world.

Exercises for Week 6

1. Take a diary and write down what you feel are your imperfections – physical, mental and emotional.

2. Once you are done, read through what you have written, and write down the opposite of it. For instance, if you wrote down, "I look a little overweight." Replace it with, "I'm in my perfect body at my ideal weight. I absolutely love my body."

3. Once you have written down a positive statement for each of your perceived imperfections. Read them out aloud – try doing it several times a day until you can infuse some conviction in it.

4. Do this exercise daily for this week and soon you will start experiencing a transformation. Once you start treating yourself differently, other people will also treat you differently.

5. The most amazing thing about this exercise is that over time (if done consistently and with persistent belief), your body will start molding into the ideal image that you have in mind. This is because after a while the subconscious mind starts embracing the idea and once the messages have reached your subconscious mind, your reality is bound to undergo a radical shift.

6. For this week, love yourself and practice affirmations to proclaim your love for yourself. Do this for at least 5-10 minutes every day. You can do it while taking a shower, while doing chores around the house, in front of the mirror or just wherever you feel like. If you start enjoying this and it starts changing your life, then don't miss out on making it an essential part of your daily routine for the rest of your life.

Conclusion

Thank you so much for taking this six-week journey with me. I hope I was able to add value to your life through my insights and experiences. If you decided to read this book in one go, then be sure to go back and go through each chapter week by week putting the exercises to practice.

I truly believe that the real value any book has to offer does not lie in the knowledge it contains but the practical wisdom it offers that one can adapt to enhance one's quality of life. I hope that you will practice the exercises and will find at least some things that work for you. I'm sure that with regular application, they will have a transformative effect in your life.

I would also suggest that you keep this book as a handy reference guide for whenever you need a little inspiration for living a more French Chic life.

Also, if you enjoyed this book, then I'd like to ask you for a favor. Would you be kind enough to leave a review for this book on Amazon? It'd be greatly appreciated!

If you are looking for inspiration to build a French Chic wardrobe and you haven't already read the first book, French Chic: The Ultimate Guide to French Fashion, Beauty and Style, then be sure to check it out on Amazon.

Thank you and good luck on your journey to a chicer life!

Made in the USA
Monee, IL
04 May 2025